The Toy Book

By JOE KAUFMAN

GOLDEN PRESS **NEW YORK**

© Copyright 1965 by Western Publishing Company, Inc. Designed and produced by Artists and Writers Press, Inc.
Printed in the U.S.A. by Western Printing and Lithographing Company. Published by Golden Press, Inc., New York.

Brown bear

My brown bear smiles.

My white boat sails.

My crayons color.

F

My blue kite flies.

Red ball

My red ball bounces.

Gray car

My gray car zooms.

Pink doll

My pink doll
sleeps.

Black engine

My black
engine
goes.

Green top

My green
top spins.

Orange
fish

My orange fish swims.

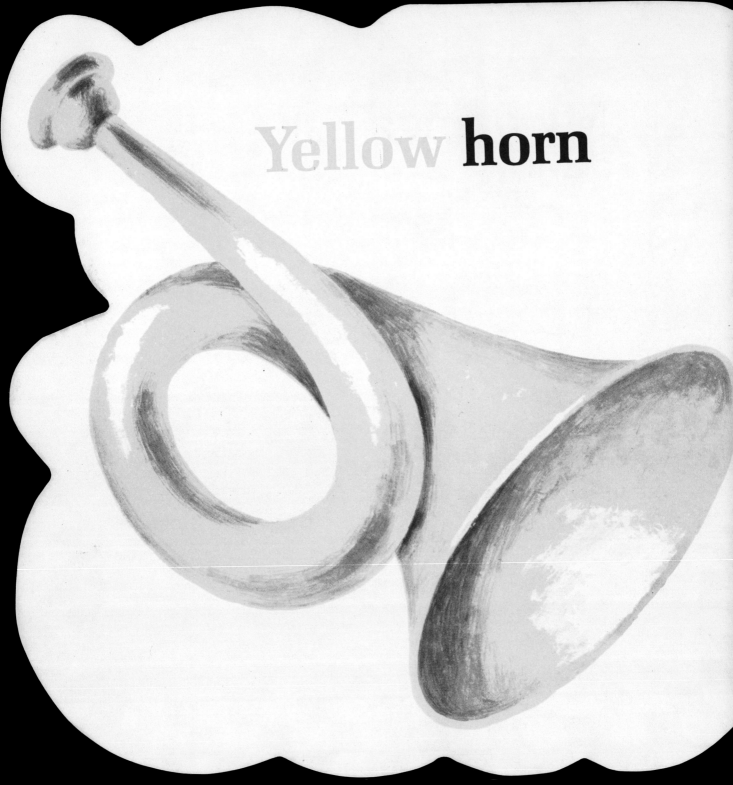

Yellow horn

My yellow horn toots.

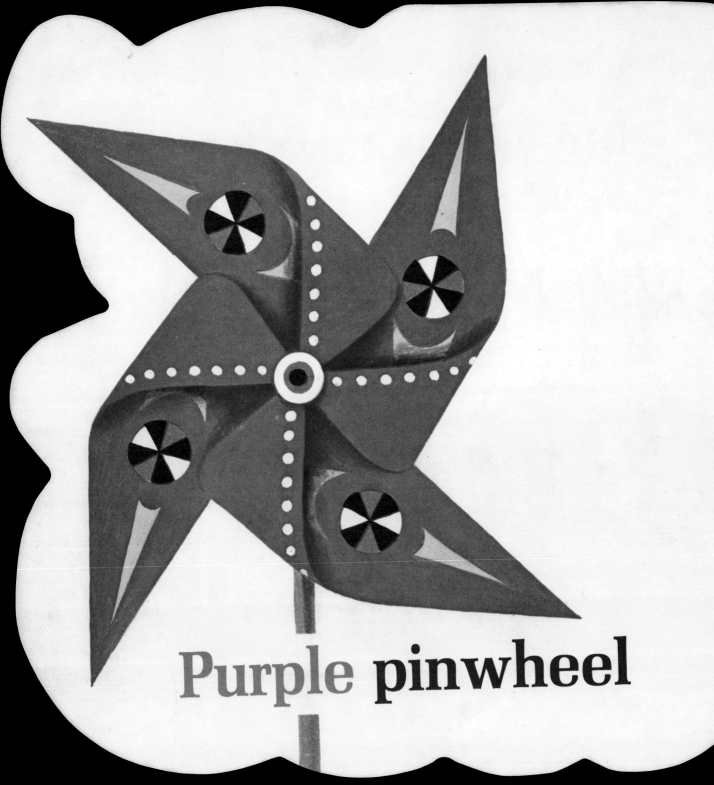

Purple pinwheel

My purple pinwheel twirls.

White
boat